Spenser St. John

Rajah Brooke

The Englishman as Ruler of an Eastern State

Spenser St. John

Rajah Brooke
The Englishman as Ruler of an Eastern State

ISBN/EAN: 9783337157890

Printed in Europe, USA, Canada, Australia, Japan

Cover: Foto ©ninafisch / pixelio.de

More available books at **www.hansebooks.com**

BUILDERS OF
GREATER BRITAIN

EDITED BY H. F. WILSON, M.A.

Barrister-at-Law
Late Fellow of Trinity College, Cambridge
Legal Assistant at the Colonial Office

BUILDERS OF GREATER BRITAIN

RAJAH BROOKE

Brooke

RAJAH BROOKE

THE ENGLISHMAN AS RULER OF AN
EASTERN STATE

BY

Sir SPENSER ST JOHN, G.C.M.G.

AUTHOR OF
'HAYTI; OR, THE BLACK REPUBLIC,'
'LIFE IN THE FORESTS OF THE FAR EAST,'
ETC.

LONDON
T. FISHER UNWIN
PATERNOSTER SQUARE
MDCCCXCIX

PREFACE ·

I HAVE undertaken to write the life of the old
Rajah, Sir James Brooke, my first and only
chief, as one of the Builders of Greater Britain.
In his case the expression must be used in its
widest sense, as, in fact, he added but an in-
appreciable fragment to the Empire, whilst at
the same time he was the cause of large
territories being included within our sphere of
influence. And if his advice had been followed,
we should not now be troubled with the restless
ambition of France in the Hindu - Chinese
regions, as his policy was to secure, by well
defined treaties, the independence of those
Asiatic States, subject, however, to the beneficent
influence of England as the Paramount Power,
an influence to be used for the good of the
governed. Sir James thoroughly understood
that Eastern princes and chiefs are at first only

influenced by fear ; the fear of the consequences
which might follow the neglect of the counsels
of the protecting State.

The plan which the Rajah endeavoured to
persuade the English Government to adopt
was to make treaties with all the independent
princes of the Eastern Archipelago, including
those States whose shores are washed by the
China Sea, as Siam, Cambodia and Annam, by
which they could cede no territory to any
foreign power without the previous consent of
England, and to establish at the capitals of the
larger States well-chosen diplomatic agents, to
encourage the native rulers not only to improve
the internal condition of their countries, but to
inculcate justice in their treatment of foreigners,
and thus avoid complications with other powers.

Sir James Brooke first attempted to carry out
this enlightened policy by concluding treaties
with the Sultans of Borneo and Sulu, to secure
these States from extinction ; the latter treaty
was not ratified, however, owing to the timidity
of a naval officer, foolishly influenced by a
clever Spanish Consul in Singapore, who took
advantage of the absence of the Rajah.   In
the forties and fifties the expansion of Great

Britain, as is well known, was looked upon with genuine alarm by many of our leading statesmen.

Sir James Brooke, however, was not destined to see the fufilment of his ideas, as a ministry came into power in 1853 which cared nothing for the Further East, and in the hope of consolidating their majority in Parliament sacrificed their noble officer to appease the clamour raised by Joseph Hume and his followers, who, like other zealots, pursued their objects regardless of all the evidence which could be brought to refute their unfounded accusations. Joseph Hume may be called a libeller by profession, who began his career by making his fortune in the East India Company's service in a very few years—a remarkable achievement; and who afterwards, when in Parliament, brought himself into notoriety by attacking first Sir Thomas Maitland, secondly Lord Torrington, and ultimately Sir James Brooke, whose shoe latchets he was unworthy to unloose.

Sir James had thus but a short career as an English official. He was named Confidential Agent in 1845, Commissioner and Consul-General in 1846, Governor of Labuan in

1847, and his return to England in 1851 practically closed his active political connection with England, though he did not resign all his offices until 1854.

But the Rajah did not thus conclude his own career ; he returned to Sarawak and devoted all his energies to the development of his adopted country, and of the neighbouring districts. I shall have to relate what extraordinary vicissitudes of fortune he had to encounter, and how after many years of conflict he emerged triumphant, to leave to his successor, Sir Charles Brooke, a small kingdom, well organised as far as Sarawak was concerned, with strongly established positions reaching to Bintulu, which have but increased in influence and in power to further the. well-being of the natives of every race and class ; and to prove to all who care to interest themselves in the subject, what a gain to humanity has resulted from the old Rajah having had the courage and the forethought to found his rule in a wild country, whose inhabitants, with few exceptions, were till then inimical to Europeans, and mostly tainted by piracy. But he argued truly that these people knew very imperfectly what Englishmen were, and he determined to show them that some, at all events, were worthy of their confidence, and could devote themselves without reserve to their welfare.

The peculiarity of the Rajah's system was to treat the natives, as far as possible, as equals ; not only equals before the law, but in society. All his followers endeavoured to imitate their chief, and succeeded in a greater or less degree, thus producing a state of good feeling in the country which was probably found nowhere else in the East, except in Perak, one of the Protected States in the Malay Peninsula, into which one of his most able assistants introduced his method of government. I am told that this good feeling, if not the old friendly intimacy between native and European, still exists to a considerable degree throughout the possessions of the present Rajah, which is highly honourable to him and to his officers.

I have not attempted to re-write my account of the Chinese Insurrection (see Chapter VI.). I wrote it when all the events were fresh in my mind, and no subsequent information has rendered it necessary to make any changes. It was a most interesting and important inci-

dent in the Rajah's career, and it fixed for
ever in the minds of his countrymen how
wise and beneficent must have been his rule
of the Malays and Dyaks, that they should
have stood by him as they did when
he appeared before them as a defeated
fugitive.

How far-seeing were the Rajah's views and
plans is proved by the fact that his successor
has found it unnecessary to change any phase
of his policy, whether political or commercial,
whether financial, agricultural or judicial ; with
the growth of the country in population and
wealth all has been of course considerably aug-
mented, but the lines on which this great
advance has been made were laid by the first
Rajah, and that this honour is due to him
no one should deny.

As there was but one Nelson, so there has
been but one Sir James Brooke. How admirable
was the simplicity of his character ! So kind
and gentle was he in manner, that the poorest,
most down-trodden native would approach him
without fear, confident that his story would be
heard with benevolent attention, and that any
wrong would, if possible, be righted. And as

for the purity of his private life, he was a bright example to all those around him.

It may be thought that I have exaggerated the grandeur of the Rajah's personality, and the great benefits he conferred on the natives, and that I have been influenced in my views by the warm friendship which existed between us. If there be any who hold this opinion, I would refer them to Mr Alfred Wallace's work, *The Malay Archipelago*, in which, after dwelling in a most appreciative manner on the Rajah's rule in Sarawak, he adds these eloquent words, 'Since these lines were written his noble spirit has passed away. But though by those who knew him not he may be sneered at as an enthusiastic adventurer, or abused as a hard-hearted despot, the universal testimony of everyone who came in contact with him in his adopted country, whether European, Malay or Dyak, will be that Rajah Brooke was a great, a wise and a good ruler, a true and faithful friend, a man to be admired for his talents, respected for his honesty and courage, and loved for his genuine hospitality, his kindness of disposition and his tenderness of heart.'

The portrait of Rajah Brooke facing the title page is taken from the picture by Sir Francis Grant, which is one of his best works. It is a most speaking likeness, and I have left it in my will to the Trustees of the National Portrait Gallery, if they will accept it.

SPENSER ST JOHN.

4 Chester Street, S.W.

Note.—I would wish to add a few words to explain why, in the course of this *Life* of Rajah Brooke, I have not dwelt on the controversy which raged for some years about the character of the Seribas and Sakarang Dyaks. The only person who, to a late period, held to his view that these tribes were not piratical was Mr Gladstone; but after reading my first *Life of Rajah Brooke*, in which I defended the policy of my old chief with all the vigour I could command, I received the following note from him, which rendered unnecessary any further discussion of the subject :—

February 25, 1880.

My dear Sir,—I thank you very much for sending me your *Life of Sir James Brooke*, which I shall be anxious to examine with care. I have myself written words about Sir James Brooke which may serve to show that the difference between us is not so wide as might be supposed, and I fully admit that what I have questioned in his acts has been accepted by his legitimate superiors, the Government and the Parliament.—I remain, yours faithfully, W. E. GLADSTONE.

His EXCELLENCY SPENSER ST JOHN.

It is as well that I should publish another letter, to show that Mr Gladstone bore me no ill-will on account of the vigorous way I had attacked him whilst defending the policy of my old chief. I had applied to Lord Granville to be sent out as Special Envoy to renew relations with the Republic of Mexico, and the following is his Lordship's reply :—

FOREIGN OFFICE, *May* 28, 1883.

MY DEAR SIR SPENSER,—Many thanks for your note. I have availed myself of your offer, mentioning it to Gladstone, who highly approved (notwithstanding the hard blows you once dealt him), and I have submitted your name to the Queen, who, I feel sure, will sanction the step.— Yours sincerely, GRANVILLE.

It is pleasant to place on record this generosity of feeling in one of our greatest statesmen, whose career has now been closed.

CONTENTS

CHAPTER IV

CHAPTER V

CHAPTER VI

CHAPTER VII

CONTENTS xxiii

CHAPTER VIII

CHAPTER IX

APPENDIX

LIST OF ILLUSTRATIONS

xxiv

Rajah Brooke

CHAPTER I

JAMES BROOKE was the second son of Mr Thomas Brooke of the Honourable East India Company's Bengal Civil Service, and of Anna Maria Stuart, his wife. Their family consisted of two sons and four daughters. One of the latter, Emma, married the Rev. F. C. Johnson, Vicar of White Lackington; another, Margaret, married the Rev. Anthony Savage; the eldest son, Henry, died unmarried after a short career in the Indian army.

Mr Thomas Brooke was the seventh in descent from Sir Thomas Vyner, who, as Lord Mayor of London, entertained Oliver Cromwell in the Guildhall in 1654; whilst his only son, Sir Robert Vyner,

A

who had taken the opposite side in those civil con-
tests, received Charles II. in the city six years
later. On the death of Sir Robert's only son
George the baronetcy became extinct, and the
family estate of Eastbury, in Essex, reverted to
the two daughters of Sir Thomas Vyner, from one
of whom, Edith, the Brooke family is derived, as
one of her descendants married a Captain Brooke,
who was Rajah Brooke's great-grandfather.[1]

Mr Thomas Brooke, though not distinguished
by remarkable talent, was a straightforward, honest
civilian, and his wife was a most lovable woman,
who gained the affections of all those with whom
she was brought into contact. She always enjoyed
the most perfect confidence of her distinguished
son. To her are addressed some of his finest
letters, in which he pours forth his generous ideas
for the promotion of the welfare of the people
whom he had been called upon to govern.

James Brooke was born on the 29th of April
1803 at Secrore, the European suburb of Benares,
and he remained in India until he was twelve
years old, when he was sent to England to the
care of Mrs Brooke, his paternal grandmother, who
had established herself in Reigate. He shortly afterwards went to Norwich Grammar School, at that
time under Dr Valpy, but he remained there only

[1] These details are taken from Miss Jacob's *Life of the Rajah of
Sarawak*, Vol. I., page 1.

a couple of years, as, after the freedom of his life
in India, discipline was irksome to him, and he ran
away home to his grandmother. I never heard him
say much about the master, but he loved and was
beloved by many of his schoolfellows, and showed
even then, by his influence over the boys, that he
was a born leader of men.

About this time his parents returned from India
and settled at Combe Grove, near Bath, where
they collected their children around them. A
private tutor was engaged to educate young Brooke,
but it could have been only for a comparatively
short time, as in 1819 he received his ensign's
commission in the 6th Madras Native Infantry, and
soon started for India. He was promoted to his
lieutenancy in 1821, and in the following year
was made a Sub-Assistant Commissary-General, a
post for which, as he used to say, he was emin-
ently unfitted.

When the war with Burmah broke out in 1824
Brooke found himself thoroughly in his element.
As the English army advanced into Assam the
general in command found himself much hampered
in his movements by the want of cavalry. Brooke
partly relieved him of this difficulty ; his offer to
raise a body of horsemen was accepted. By the
orders of the general he called for recruits, who could
ride, from the different regiments, and soon had
under him an efficient body of men, who under-

took scouting duties. He found it difficult to keep them in hand, for the moment they saw an enemy they would charge, and then scatter in every direction where they thought a Burmese might be concealed.

During an action in January 1825 he performed very efficient service with his irregular cavalry, charging wherever any body of Burmese collected. He received the thanks of the general, and his conduct was mentioned in despatches as 'most conspicuous.' Two days later occurred an instance of what is almost unknown in our army. A company of native troops had been ordered to attack a stockade manned by Burmese; the English officer in command advanced until, on turning a clump of trees, he came well under fire; then, losing his nerve, he bolted into the jungle. Brooke arrived at that moment, saw the infantry wavering, threw himself from his horse, assumed the command, and thus encouraged they charged the stockade, but Brooke literally 'foremost, fighting fell.' Seeing their leader fall, the men were again about to retreat, when Colonel Richards, advancing with reinforcements, restored the fight, and in a few minutes the place was taken, though with heavy loss. No attempts were ever made to turn these strong stockades, and thus the army suffered severely and to no purpose.

I have often heard Sir James Brooke tell the

story. He had been sent out to reconnoitre; found the enemy strongly posted, and suspecting an ambuscade, galloped back to warn his superior officer, but too late, as firing had already commenced, and the infantry, without a leader, were confused. He placed himself at their head, but as he charged he felt a thud, and fell, losing all consciousness. After the action was over, his colonel, who had seen him fall, inquired about young Brooke, and was told that he was dead; but examining the fallen officer himself, found him still alive and had him removed to hospital. A slug had lodged in his lungs, and for months he lay between life and death. It was not, in fact, until August that he was strong enough to be removed, and then only in a canoe. He was paddled down a branch of the Bramapootra, rarely suffering from pain, but gazing pensively at the fast-running stream and the fine jungle that lined its banks; in after life it seemed to him as a dream.

On the Medical Board at Calcutta reporting that a change of climate was necessary, he was given a long furlough. He returned to England and joined his family at Bath. The voyage did him some good, but the wound continued very troublesome, and at times it appeared as if he could not recover. After the slug had been extracted, however, he gradually got better, so that in July 1829 he was enabled to embark on board the Company's ship

Carn Brae; but fate was against his again joining
the Indian army. This vessel was wrecked, and
when, in the following March, he sailed for the
East on board the *Huntley Castle,* she was so
delayed by bad weather, that when she called in
at Madras Brooke found that he could not join
his regiment before the legal expiration of his
leave. He consequently resigned the service and
proceeded in the *Huntley Castle* to China.

Brooke never cared much for the East India
Company's service, and as he had formed friendships
on board the *Huntley Castle* he preferred continuing in
her to remaining idle in India awaiting the Directors'
decision, which, even if favourable, could scarcely arrive
before twelve months had expired. The decision was
favourable ; but as young Brooke had in the meantime
left Madras the matter dropped. The Indiaman first
touched at the Island of Penang, one of the Straits
Settlements, and here Brooke had an opportunity of
seeing what lovely islands there were in the Further
East. It is not necessary to dwell on this voyage, as
nothing of importance occurred during it ; but his stay
in China made a deep impression on Brooke's mind.
He saw how the Chinese ill-treated and bullied our
countrymen, and how the East India Company submitted to every insult in order not to imperil their trade.

After the usual stay in the Canton River, the
Huntley Castle returned to England, and Brooke
found himself at home with no employment whatever.

He formed many projects; the favourite one, which he had discussed with the officers of the *Huntley Castle*, was to purchase a ship, load her with suitable goods, and sail for China or the adjacent markets. But as none of the friends had any capital, Brooke confided their views to his father, and naturally met with the objection that his son was not a trader and never could become one. However, in the end, the young fellow prevailed. The brig *Findlay* was bought, laden with goods, and with his partner, Kennedy, formerly of the *Huntley Castle*, and his friend, Harry Wright, also of the same vessel, he set sail for the Further East. This voyage was not destined to be a success. Brooke wished to introduce on board the easy discipline of a yacht, whilst Kennedy, who was captain, went to the other extreme and would insist upon the severe discipline of the navy, without its safeguards. Differences soon arose, and as they found trade by interlopers was not encouraged, Brooke went to see Mr Jardine, of the firm of Messrs Jardine, Matheson & Company, and laid the case before him. The shrewd man of business could not but smile at the idea of this elegant young soldier managing a trading speculation. He, however, agreed to buy vessel and cargo, and told the partners they had better leave the matter in his hands. No objection was raised, and Mr Jardine so judiciously invested in silks the amount he had arranged to pay, that in the end comparatively little loss accrued, none of which was allowed by Brooke to fall on Kennedy.

On his return to England Brooke wearied of
continued leisure, and although he yachted about the
Southern Coast and the Channel Islands, he longed
for some sphere of action which could bring his great
abilities into play. The death of his father, in
December 1835, gave him complete independence.
The fortune left was sufficient to provide for his
wife, and to give to each of his children £30,000.
Brooke now decided to carry out the plan he had
formed since his first voyage to China, which was to
buy a small vessel and start on a voyage of discovery.
But this time there were to be no partners and no
trade ; he intended to be complete master in his own
ship. He ultimately fixed his choice on the *Royalist*,
a schooner yacht of about 142 tons burden. He was
delighted with his purchase, and soon tried her
qualifications by starting in the autumn of 1836 for
a cruise in the Mediterranean. There he visited
most of the principal cities, including Constantinople,
which in after years afforded him a constant subject of
conversation with the Malays, who interested themselves in every detail of his visit. 'Roum' to them is
still the great city where dwells the head of the
Mohammedan religion.[1] Among those who accompanied him on this cruise was his nephew, John Brooke

---

[1] When I first went to live in Brunei, the Sultan of Borneo's capital,
there was living there an old haji who was visiting Egypt at the time
of Buonaparte's invasion, and who remembered well the Battle of the
Nile and the subsequent expulsion of the French by the English.

Johnson, afterwards known as Captain Brooke, and also John Templer, who was then and for many years afterwards one of his warm friends and enthusiastic admirers.

Though determined to make a voyage of discovery in the Eastern Archipelago, Brooke was not able to leave England till December 1838. He employed all his spare time in studying the subject, finding out what was already known, and drawing attention to his plans by a memoir he wrote on Borneo and the neighbouring islands, summaries of which were published in the *Athenæum* and in the *Journal* of the Geographical Society. He felt a great admiration for Sir Stamford Raffles, and ardently desired to carry out his views in dealing with the peoples of the Further East.

How well Brooke sums up the feelings which prompted him to undertake what was in every respect a perilous enterprise ! 'Could I carry my vessel to places where the keel of European ship never before ploughed the waters ; could I plant my foot where white man's foot had never before been ; could I gaze upon scenes which educated eyes had never looked on, see man in the rudest state of nature, I should be content without looking to further rewards.'

It is difficult, even under the most favourable circumstances, to convey to the mind of a reader an exact portrait of the man whose deeds you desire to chronicle ; but as I lived for nearly twenty years with James Brooke, I feel I know him well in all his strength and his weakness. Let me try to describe him. He stood about five feet ten inches in height; he had an open, handsome countenance; an active, supple frame; a daring courage that no danger could daunt; a sweet, affectionate disposition which endeared him to all who knew him well. Those whom he attended in sickness could never forget his almost womanly tenderness, and those who attended him, his courageous endurance. His power of attaching both friends and followers was unrivalled, and this extended to nearly every native with whom he came in contact. His few failings were his too great frankness, his readiness to believe that men were what they professed to be, or should have been, and (for a short time in latter years) that the unsophisticated lower classes were more to be trusted and relied on than those above them in birth and education. His only weaknesses were, in truth, such as arose from his great goodness of heart and his confiding nature.

No painter ever succeeded better in conveying a man's self into a portrait than Sir Francis Grant in his picture of Sir James Brooke. I have it now before me, and all I have said of his appearance may be seen at a glance. Although thirty years have passed since we lost him, he remains as much enshrined as ever in the hearts of his few surviving friends.

This brief preliminary chapter ended, I will now describe Brooke's voyage to Borneo, and the events which succeeded that remarkable undertaking.

CHAPTER II

EXPEDITION TO BORNEO—FIRST VISIT TO SARAWAK—
VOYAGE TO CELEBES—SECOND VISIT TO SARAWAK
—JOINS MUDA HASSIM'S ARMY—BROOKE'S AC-
COUNT OF THE PROGRESS OF THE CIVIL WAR—
IT IS ENDED UNDER THE INFLUENCE OF HIS
ACTIVE INTERFERENCE—HE SAVES THE LIVES OF
THE REBEL CHIEFS

BROOKE sailed from Devonport on December 16,
1838, in the *Royalist*, belonging to the Royal Yacht
Squadron, which, in foreign ports, admitted her to the
same privileges as a ship of war, and enabled her to carry
a white ensign. As the *Royalist* is still an historic
character in the Eastern Archipelago, I must let the
owner describe her as she was in 1838. 'She sails
fast; is conveniently fitted up; is armed with six
six-pounders, and a number of swords and small arms
of all sorts; carries four boats and provisions for four
months. Her principal defect is being too sharp in
the floor. She is a good sea boat, and as well calculated
for the service as could be desired. Most of the
hands have been with me for three years, and the
rest are highly recommended.'

11

Whilst the *Royalist* is speeding on prosperously towards Singapore, and calling at Rio Janeiro and the Cape, let me sum up in a few words the object of the voyage.

The memorandum [1] which Brooke drew up on the then state of the Indian Archipelago (1838), shows how carefully he had studied the whole subject. He first expounds the policy which England should follow if she wished to recover the position which she wantonly threw away after the peace of 1815; he then explains what he proposed to do for the furtherance of our knowledge of Borneo and the other great islands to the East. Circumstances, however, as he anticipated might be the case, made him change the direction of his first local voyage.

The *Royalist* arrived in Singapore in May 1839, and remained at that port till the end of July, refitting and preparing for future work. There Brooke received news which induced him to give up for the present the proposed voyage to Marudu Bay, the northernmost district of Borneo, and visit Sarawak instead. Rajah Muda Hassim, uncle to the Sultan of Brunei, was then residing there, and being of a kindly disposition, had taken care of the crew of a shipwrecked English vessel, and sent the men in safety to Singapore. This unlooked-for conduct on the part of a Malay chief roused the interest of the Singapore merchants, and Brooke was requested to

[1] *See* Appendix.

call in at Sarawak and deliver to the Malay prince a
letter and presents from the Chamber of Commerce.

This was a fortunate diversion of his voyage, as
at that time Marudu was governed by a notorious
pirate chief. The bay was a rendezvous for some of
the most daring marauders in the Archipelago, and
nothing could have been done there to further our
knowledge of the interior.

All being ready, and the crew strengthened by
eight Singapore Malay seamen,[1] athletic fellows, capital
at the oar, and to save the white men the work of
wooding and watering, the *Royalist* sailed for Borneo
on the 27th of July, and in five days was anchored
off the coast of Sambas. All the charts were found
to be wrong, so that every care had to be taken
whilst working up the coast. A running survey
was made, and on the 11th August Brooke found
himself at the mouth of the Sarawak river.

When Brooke first arrived in Borneo, the Sultan
Omar Ali claimed all the coast from the capital to
Tanjong Datu, whilst further south was Sambas,
under the influence of the Dutch; but the rule of
Omar Ali was little more than nominal, as each chief
in the different districts exercised almost unlimited
power, and paid little or no tribute to the central
Government.

At the time of Brooke's first visit to Sarawak the

[1] I knew one of them, Subu, the favourite of every foreigner in
Sarawak.

Malays of the country had broken out into revolt against the oppressive rule of Pangeran Makota, Governor of the district, and fearing that they might call in the aid of the Sambas Malays, and thus place the country under the control of the Dutch, the Sultan sent down Rajah Muda Hassim, his uncle and heir-presumptive, to endeavour to stifle the rebellion ; but three years had passed, and he had done nothing. He could prevent the rebels from communicating with the sea, but he was powerless in the interior.

On hearing of the arrival of the *Royalist* at the mouth of the river, Muda Hassim despatched a deputation to welcome the stranger and invite him to the capital—rather a grand name for a small village. Brooke soon got his vessel under weigh, and proceeded up the Sarawak, and after one slight mishap, anchored the next day opposite the rajah's house, and saluted his flag with twenty-one guns.

Muda Hassim received Brooke in state, and the interview is thus described : 'The rajah was seated in his hall of audience, which, outside, is nothing but a large shed, erected on piles, but within decorated with taste. Chairs were arranged on either side of the ruler, who occupied the head seat. Our party were placed on one hand, and on the other sat his brother Mahommed, and Makota and some other of the principal chiefs, whilst immediately behind him his twelve younger brothers were seated. The dress of Muda Hassim was simple, but of rich material, and

most of the principal men were well, and even superbly
dressed. His countenance is plain, but intelligent and
highly pleasing, and his manners perfectly easy. His
reception was kind, and, I am given to understand,
highly flattering. We sat, however, trammelled by
the formalities of state, and our conversation did not
extend beyond kind inquiries and professions of friendship.' Brooke's next interview was more informal,
and closer relations were established, which encouraged
him to send his interpreter, Mr Williamson, to ask
permission to visit the Dyaks. This was readily
granted, but before commencing his explorations,
he received a private visit from Pangeran Makota.
He was probably the most intelligent Malay whom
we ever met in Borneo, frank and open in manner,
but looked upon as the most cunning of the rajah's
advisers. He was much puzzled, as were indeed all
the nobles, as to the true object of Brooke's visit to
Borneo, and confident in his power, determined to
find it out. And though Brooke had in reality no
object but geographical discovery, he could not convince his guest of that fact, who scented some deep
intrigue under the guise of a harmless visit.

Brooke now took advantage of the rajah's permission
to explore some of the neighbouring rivers, and he was
shown first the fine agricultural district of Samarahan,
but only met Malays. His next visit was to the
Dyak tribe of Sibuyows, who lived on the river
Lundu, which discharged its waters not many miles

from Cape Datu, the southern boundary of Borneo proper.

From Tanjong Datu, as far as the river Rejang, the interior populations are called Dyaks — Land or Sea Dyaks—the former, a quiet, agricultural people, living in the far interior, plundered and oppressed by the Malays ; they are to be found in Sarawak, Samarahan and Sadong. The Sea Dyaks were much more numerous, and though under the influence of the Malays and Arab adventurers, were too powerful ever to be ill-treated. They occupied the districts of Seribas and Batang Lupar, and those on the left bank of the Rejang, with a few scattered villages in other parts, such as this Sibuyow tribe on the Lundu.

The chief of this branch of the Sea Dyaks, the Orang Kaya Tumangong, was always a great favourite of the English officers in Sarawak. His was the first tribe that Brooke visited, and he then formed a high opinion of the brave man and his gallant sons, who were faithful unto death, and who were always the foremost when any fighting was on hand.

The village they occupied was, in fact, but one huge house, nearly six hundred feet in length, and the inner half divided into fifty separate residences for the fifty families that constituted the tribe. The front half of this long building was an open space, which was used by the inhabitants during the day for every species of work, and at night was occupied by the widowers,

bachelors and boys as their bedroom. The Sea
Dyaks are much cleaner than the Land Dyaks, and
the girls of Sakarang, for instance, looked as well
washed as any of their sisters in May Fair.

The distinction of Land and Sea Dyaks was due
to the fact that the former never ventured near the
salt water, whilst the latter boldly pushed out to sea
in their light bangkongs or war boats, and cruised
along at least two thousand miles of coast. When the
Royalist first arrived in Sarawak the majority of the
Sea Dyaks were piratically inclined. This practice
arose in all probability from their inter-tribal wars—
the Scribas against the Lingas and Sibuyows—and from
their custom of seeking heads — almost a religious
observance. When a party of young men went out to
search for the means of marrying, and had failed to
secure the heads of enemies, we can easily imagine
their not being too particular about killing any weaker
party they might meet, even if they were not enemies,
and, finding it met with no retaliation, continuing the
practice. In this they were encouraged by the Malay
chiefs who lived among them, and who obtained, on
easy terms, the women and children captives who fell
into the hands of the Dyak raiders. Although the
Linga and Sibuyow branches of the Sea Dyaks hunted
for heads, they were the heads of their enemies, whilst
the Scribas, and, in a lesser degree, the Sea Dyaks of
the Sakarang and the Rejang spared no one they
could overcome.

B

Brooke's next visit was to the river Sadong, to the north-east of Sarawak, and there he met Sherif Sahib, a great encourager of piracy of every kind. Sometimes he received the Lanuns,[1] the boldest marauders who ever invested the Far Eastern seas, bought their captives and supplied them with food, whilst at others he would aid the Seribas and Sakarangs in their forays on the almost defenceless tribes of the interior, or share their plunder acquired on the coasts of the Dutch possessions.

Finding that the rebellion in the interior of the Sarawak would prevent him from visiting it, Brooke decided to return to Singapore. After a friendly parting with Muda Hassim, whose last words were, 'Do not forget me,' the *Royalist* fell down the river. The night before Brooke had settled to sail he was joined by a small Sarawak boat with a dozen men, who were to pilot him out ; but about midnight shouts were heard from the shore of 'Dyak ! Dyak' ! In an instant a blue light was burnt on board the yacht and a gun fired, and then there came a dead silence. Brooke sprang into a boat and pushed off to the Malay prahu, to find half the crew wounded. It seemed that a cruising party of Seribas Dyaks had no doubt seen the fire lighted on the shore, and had noiselessly floated up with the flood tide and attacked the Malays, not

[1] The Lanuns came from the great island of Mindanau, in the Southern Philippines, which was a nominal possession of Spain, and cruised in well-armed vessels.

observing in the dark night the *Royalist* at anchor. This occurrence showed how necessary it was to be on one's guard at all times.

The news brought by Brooke was well received in Singapore, as it opened up a new country to British commerce, and prevented the Dutch gaining a footing there, with their vexatious trade regulations, which practically debarred native vessels from visiting British ports.

As the Rajah Muda Hassim had assured his English visitor that the rebellion in the interior of Sarawak would collapse before the next fine season, he decided to pass the interval in visiting Celebes, a most attractive island, then but imperfectly known.

No part of Brooke's journals is more interesting than the account of his experiences in Bugis land. They are, however, simple travels, without many personal incidents to be noted ; but here, as elsewhere, he acquired the same ascendency over the natives, and the memory of his visit remained impressed on the minds of the Bugis rulers, who followed his advice in regulating their kingdoms, and especially listened to his counsels when he pointed out the danger of entering into armed conflict with their Dutch neighbours.

The following observations extracted from Brooke's journals are remarkable : 'I must mention the effect of European domination in the Archipelago. The first voyagers from the West found

the natives rich and powerful, with strong established governments and a thriving trade. The
rapacious European has reduced them to their
present position. Their governments have been
broken up, the old states decomposed by treachery,
bribery and intrigue, their possessions snatched from
them under flimsy pretences, their trade restricted,
their vices encouraged, their virtues repressed, and
their energies paralysed or rendered desperate, till
there is every reason to fear the gradual extinction
of the Malay.   Let these considerations, fairly re-
flected on and enlarged, be presented to the candid
and liberal mind, and I think that, however strong
the present prepossessions, they will shake the belief
in the advantages to be gained by European ascendency, as it has heretofore been conducted, and will
convince the most sceptical of the miseries immediately and prospectively flowing from European rule
as generally constituted.'

The above observations naturally apply to the
Dutch and Spanish systems, which at that time
alone had sway in the Archipelago, as England,
with its small trading depots, did not actively inter-
fere with the native princes. Yet it must be confessed that Borneo proper, which had generally escaped
interference from their European neighbours, fell from
a position fairly important to the most degraded state,
entirely owing to the incapacity of its native rulers
and not to outside influences.

The visits to Sarawak and Celebes tended to confirm Brooke's convictions that, if England would but act on a settled plan and on a sufficient scale, she could still save and develop the independent native states, without any necessity of occupying them.

In the year 1776 the Sultan of Sulu ceded to England all his possessions in the north of Borneo, and the East India Company formed a small settlement on the Island of Balambangan; this being on a very inefficient scale, was easily surprised by pirates and destroyed. Later on another attempt was made by the Company to establish themselves on the island, but it was soon abandoned.

Brooke, after carefully studying the subject, came to the same conclusion as Sir Stamford Raffles and Colonel Farquhar had done before him, that it was a mistake to take small islands; but that, on the contrary, this country should establish a settlement on the mainland of Borneo. As all the independent states of the Archipelago are filled with a maritime population, islands are not so safe from attack as the mainland, where the interior population is rarely warlike. He recommended that England should take possession of Marudu Bay, establish herself strongly there, be constantly supported by the navy, and from thence the Governor, with diplomatic powers, could visit all the independent chiefs and make such treaties with them as would prevent their being absorbed by other European States. His policy was of the most liberal kind ; he would have sought no exclusive trade privileges, but he would have preserved their political independence. He would have established in the more important states carefully - selected English agents, to encourage the chiefs in useful reforms and to prevent restrictions on commerce. On the mainland he would not have instantly established English rule, except in a well-chosen, central spot, and there he would have awaited the invitation of the chiefs to send an English officer to aid them in governing.

Had this great plan been executed on a suitable scale Brooke's name would have been enshrined among the greatest builders of the British Empire. It is not too late even now ; but where shall we find another Brooke to carry it out ? North Borneo is at present under the protection of Great Britain, but it is owned and administered by a Chartered Company, and in these days cannot, under such conditions, hold the same position as a Crown colony.

The time seems propitious. The Spaniards have lost their hold over the Philippines, and Sulu and the great island of Mindanau will soon be free from their depressing influence ; even the Dutch are acting on a more enlightened system, which would be encouraged, if England took an active interest in the Archipelago. The North Borneo Company would

scarcely refuse a proposal to place the country under
our direct rule, and with another Sir Hugh Low
it might be made a valuable possession, and would
gradually dominate the whole of the Archipelago.

The Philippines will now be governed by one of
the most progressive nations in the world, and the
effect of their rule will be far-reaching. It would
appear to be advisable that Great Britain should
simultaneously take over North Borneo, as the conditions heretofore existing have so completely changed.

From Celebes Brooke returned to Singapore to
refit. His plans were to visit Borneo again, then
proceed to Manila, and so home by Cape Horn. He
arrived at our settlement in May, left it again in
August, and reached Sarawak on the 29th, to find
himself cordially received by Muda Hassim. The
war was not over, nor was the end of it in sight.
A few half-starved Dyaks had deserted the Sarawak
Malays, and come into the Bornean camp to be fed;
but the route to Sambas was still open, and it was
suspected that supplies were furnished by the Sultan
of Sambas, who coveted the territory.

After considerable discussion and consideration,
Brooke thought he would visit the headquarters of
the army which was supposed to be besieging the
enemy; but he found it seven miles below the
principal hostile fort. The spot was called Ledah
Tanah, or the tongue of land, where the two
branches of the river meet. It was the site of the

old capital, and even when I was there some ten
years later the iron-wood posts of the houses still
existed, untouched by time, though over sixty years
in use. As Brooke expected, Makota, at the head
of the army, was doing nothing, and as he rejected
the advice of his white visitor, and seemed determined
not to advance nearer to the enemy, Brooke returned
to Sarawak, and even announced his departure, as
the North-East monsoon was coming on, and he did
not wish to face it on his voyage to Manila. However, Muda Hassim appeared to feel his departure so
acutely, that his heart smote him, and he agreed to
visit the army once more, particularly as the Land
Dyaks were now really leaving the rebels and joining
the Bornean forces. He therefore returned to the
camp, and by his energy compelled Makota to act.
The stockade at Ledah Tanah was pulled down and
moved to within a mile of the enemy's chief fort,
Balidah, and gradually stockade after stockade was
built, until the most commanding one was erected
within three hundred yards of the hostile fort. Brooke
sent to the yacht for two six-pounders and a sufficient
supply of ammunition, and, with the aid of his men,
soon battered down the weak defences of the enemy,
and then proposed an assault. But this bold advice
was looked upon as insanity, and though promises to
advance were freely given, when it came to action
they all hung back. At length, wearied with this pro-
crastination, Brooke, in spite of the entreaties of all

the native chiefs, embarked his guns and returned to the *Royalist*, and sent word to the rajah that his stay was utterly useless; but when Muda Hassim heard the decision, 'his deep regret was so visible that even all the self-command of the native could not disguise it. He begged, he entreated me to stay, and offered me the country, its government and its trade, if I would only stop and not desert him.'

Though Brooke could not accept the grant then, as it would have been extracted from the rajah's deep distress, he agreed to return to the army; and once more the guns were embarked in the boats, and every man who could be spared from the *Royalist* accompanied Brooke to the front. There he met Budrudin, Muda Hassim's favourite brother, with whom he soon contracted a friendship which ended only with the Malay prince's life. He was brave, frank and intelligent; he quickly appreciated the noble character of the white leader of men, and ever after he fully trusted him.

The episodes of the closing campaign of this civil war were so amusing, that although the story has been published several times, I cannot refrain from repeating it again in the words of the English chief.[1]

'On the 10th December we reached the fleet and disembarked our guns, taking up our residence in a house, or rather shed, close to the water. The

[1] *Voyage of the Dido*, Vol. I., page 172, *et seq.*

rajah's brother, Pangeran Budrudin, was with the
army, and I found him ready and willing to urge
upon the other indolent pangerans the proposals I
made for vigorous hostilities. We found the grand
army in a state of torpor, eating, drinking and walking
up to the forts and back again daily ; but having built
these imposing structures, and their appearance not
driving the enemy away, they were at a loss what
to do next, or how to proceed. On my arrival, I
once more insisted on mounting the guns in our
old forts, and assaulting Balidah under their fire.
Makota's timidity and vacillation were too apparent ;
but in consequence of Budrudin's overawing presence
he was obliged, from shame, to yield his assent. The
order for the attack was fixed as follows : our party
of ten (leaving six to serve the guns) were to be
headed by myself. Budrudin, Makota, Subtu and
all the lesser chiefs were to lead their followers,
from sixty to eighty in number, by the same route,
whilst fifty or more Chinese, under their captain, were
to assault by another path to their left. Makota was
to make the paths as near as possible to Balidah, with
his Dyaks, who were to extract the sudas and fill up
the holes. The guns having been mounted, and their
range ascertained the previous evening, we ascended
to the fort about eight a.m., and at ten opened our fire
and kept it up for an hour. The effect was severe.
Every shot told upon their thin defences of wood,
which fell in many places so as to leave storming

breaches. Part of the roof was cut away and tumbled down, and the shower of grape and canister rattled so as to prevent their returning our fire, except from a stray rifle. At mid-day the forces reached the fort, and it was then discovered that Makota had neglected to make any road because it rained the night before! It was evident that the rebels had gained information of our intentions as they had erected a fringe of bamboo along their defences on the very spot we had agreed to mount. Makota fancied the want of a road would delay the attack; but I well knew that delay was equivalent to failure, and so it was at once agreed that we should advance without any path. The poor man's cunning and resources were now nearly at an end. He could not refuse to accompany us, but his courage could not be brought to the point, and pale and embarrassed he retired. Everything was ready—Budrudin, the Capitan China and myself, at the head of our men— when he once more appeared, and raised a subtle point of etiquette, which answered his purpose. He represented to Budrudin that the Malays were unanimously of opinion that the rajah's brother could not expose himself in an assault; that the dread of the rajah's indignation far exceeded their dread of death; and in case any accident happened to him, his brother's fury would fall on them. Budrudin was angry, I was angry too, and the doctor most angry of all; but anger was unavailing. It was clear

they did not intend to do anything in earnest ; and
after much discussion, in which Budrudin insisted if
I went he should likewise go, and the Malays insisted
that if he went they would not go, it was resolved
that we should serve the guns, whilst Abong Mia
and the Chinese, not under the captain, should
proceed to the assault. But its fate was sealed, and
Makota had gained his object; for neither he nor
Subtu thought of exposing themselves to a single
shot. Our artillery opened and was beautifully
served. The hostile forces attempted to advance, but
our fire completely subdued them, as only three rifles
answered us, by one of which a seaman was wounded
in the hand, but not seriously. Two-thirds of the way
the storming party proceeded without the hostile army
being aware of their advance, and they might have
reached the very foot of the hill without being discovered, had not Abong Mia, from excess of piety
and rashness, began most loudly to say his prayers.
The three rifles began then to play on them. One
Chinaman was killed, the whole halted, the prayers
were more vehement than ever, and after squatting
under cover of the jungle for some time they all
returned. It was only what I expected, but I was
greatly annoyed by their cowardice and treachery—
treachery to their own cause. One lesson, however,
I learnt, and that was, that had I assaulted with our
small party, we should assuredly have been victimised.
The very evening of the failure the rajah came

up the river. I would not see him, and only heard
that the chiefs got severely reprimanded ; but the
effects of reprimand are lost where cowardice is
stronger than shame. Inactivity followed, two or
three useless forts were built, and Budrudin, much
to my regret and to the detriment of the cause,
was recalled.

'Amongst the straggling arrivals I may mention
Pangeran Dallam, with a number of men, consisting
of the Orang Bintulu, Meri, Muka and Kayan Dyaks
from the interior. Our house, or, as it originally stood,
our shed, deserves a brief record. It was about twenty
feet long, with a loose floor of reeds and an attap or
palm-leaf roof. It served us for some time, but the
attempts at theft obliged us to fence it in and
divide it into apartments—one at the end served for
Middleton, Williamson and myself. Adjoining it was
the storeroom and hospital, and the other extreme
belonged to the seamen. Our improvements kept
pace with our necessities. Theft induced us to shut
in our house at the sides, and the unevenness of the
reeds suggested the advantage of laying a floor of the
bark of trees over them, which, with mats over all,
rendered our domicile far from uncomfortable. Our
forts gradually extended to the back of the enemy's
town, on a ridge of swelling ground, whilst they
kept pace with us on the same side of the river on
the low ground. The inactivity of our troops had
long become a by-word amongst us. It was, indeed,

truly vexatious, but it was in vain to urge them on, in vain to offer assistance, in vain to propose a joint attack, or even to seek support at their hands ; promises were to be had in plenty, but performances never.

'At length our leaders resolved on building a fort at Sekundis, thus outflanking the enemy and gaining the command of the upper course of the river. The post was certainly an important one, and in consequence they set about it with the happy indifference which characterises their proceedings. Pangeran Illudin (the most active amongst them) had the building of the fort, assisted by the Orang Kaya Tumangong of Lundu. Makota, Subtu and others were at the next fort, and by chance I was there likewise ; for it seemed to be little apprehended that any interruption would take place, as the Chinese and the greater part of the Malays had been left in the boats. When the fort commenced, however, the enemy crossed the river and divided into two bodies, the one keeping in check the party at Pangeran Gapoor's fort, whilst the other made an attack on the works. The ground was not unfavourable for their purpose, for Pangeran Gapoor's fort was separated from Sekundis by a belt of thick wood which reached down to the river's edge. Sekundis itself, however, stood on clear ground, as did Gapoor's fort. I was with Makota at the latter when the enemy approached through the jungle. The two parties were within easy speaking distance, challenging and threatening each other, but the thickness of the jungle prevented our seeing or penetrating to them. When this body had advanced, the real attack commenced on Sekundis with a fire of musketry, and I was about to proceed to the scene, but was detained by Makota, who assured me there were plenty of men, and that it was nothing at all. As the musketry became thicker, I had my doubts when a Dyak came running through the jungle, and with gestures of impatience and anxiety begged me to assist the party attacked. He had been sent by my old friend the Tumangong of Lundu, to say they could not hold the post unless supported. In spite of Makota's remonstrances, I struck into the jungle, winded through the narrow path, and, after crossing an ugly stream, emerged on the clear ground. The sight was a pretty one. To the right was the unfinished stockade, defended by the Tumangong ; to the left, at the edge of the forest, about twelve or fifteen of our party, commanded by Illudin, whilst the enemy were stretched along between the points, and kept up a sharp-shooting from the hollow ground on the bank of the river. They fired and loaded and fired, and had gradually advanced on the stockade, as the ammunition of our party failed ; and as we emerged from the jungle, they were within twenty or five-and-twenty yards of the defence. A glance immediately showed me the advantage of our position,

and I charged with my Englishmen across the padi
field, and the instant we appeared on the ridge above
the river, in the hollows of which the rebels were
seeking protection, their rout was complete. They
scampered off in every direction, whilst the Dyaks
and Malays pushed them into the river. Our victory
was decisive and bloodless ; the scene was changed in
an instant, and the defeated foe lost arms and ammunition either on the field of battle or in the river, and our
exulting conquerors set no bounds to their triumph.

'I cannot omit to mention the name of Si Tundu,
a Lanun, the only native who charged with us.
His appearance and dress were most striking, the
latter being entirely of red, bound round the waist,
arms, forehead, etc., with gold ornaments, and in
his hand his formidable Bajuk sword. He danced,
or rather galloped, across the field close to me, and,
mixing with the enemy, was about to despatch a
haji, or priest, who was prostrate before him, when
one of our people interposed, and saved him by
stating that he was a companion of our own. The
Lundu Dyaks were very thankful for our support,
our praises were loudly sung, and the stockade was
concluded. After the rout, Makota, Subtu and Abong
Mia arrived on the field ; the last, with forty followers,
had ventured half way before the firing ceased, but
the detachment, under a paltry subterfuge, halted so
as not to be in time. The enemy might have had
fifty men at the attack. The defending party con-

sisted of about the same number, but the Dyaks had very few muskets. I had a dozen Englishmen, Subu, one of our Singapore boatmen, and Si Tundu. Sekundis was a great point gained, as it hindered the enemy from ascending the river and seeking supplies.

'Makota, Subtu and the whole tribe arrived as soon as their safety from danger allowed, and none were louder in their own praise, but, nevertheless, their countenances evinced some sense of shame, which they endeavoured to disguise by the use of their tongues. The Chinese came really to afford assistance, but too late. We remained until the stockade of Sekundis was finished, while the enemy kept up a wasteful fire from the opposite side of the river, which did no harm.

'The next great object was to follow up the advantage by crossing the stream, but day after day some fresh excuse brought on fresh delay, and Makota built a new fort and made a new road within a hundred yards of our old position. I cannot detail further our proceedings for many days, which consisted, on my part, in efforts to get something done, and on the others, a close adherence to the old system of promising everything and doing nothing. The Chinese, like the Malays, refused to act ; but on their part it was not fear, but disinclination. By degrees, however, the preparations for the new fort were complete, and I had gradually gained over a party of the natives to my views ; and, indeed, amongst the Malays,

c

the bravest of them had joined themselves to us, and what was better, we had Datu Pangerang and thirteen Illanuns, and the Capitan China allowed me to take his men whenever I wanted them. My weight and consequence was increased, and I rarely moved now without a long train of followers. The next step, whilst crossing the river was uncertain, was to take my guns up to Gapoor's fort, which was about six or seven hundred yards from the town, and half the distance from a rebel fort on the river's bank.

'Panglima Rajah, the day after our guns were in battery, took it into his head to build a fort on the river's side, close to the town in front, and between two of the enemy's forts. It was a bold undertaking for the old man after six weeks of uninterrupted repose. At night, the wood being prepared, the party moved down, and worked so silently that they were not discovered till their defence was nearly finished, when the enemy commenced a general firing from all their forts, returned by a similar firing from all ours, none of the parties being quite clear what they were firing at or about, and the hottest from either party being equally harmless. We were at the time about going to bed in our habitation, but expecting some reverse I set off to the stockade where our guns were placed, and opened a fire upon the town and the stockade near us, till the enemy's fire gradually slackened and died away. We then re-

turned, and in the morning were greeted with the
pleasing news that they had burned and deserted five
of their forts, and left us sole occupants of the left
bank of the river. The same day, going through the
jungle to see one of these deserted forts, we came
upon a party of the enemy, and had a brief skirmish
with them before they took to flight. Nothing can
be more unpleasant to a European than this bush-
fighting, where he scarce sees a foe, whilst he is well
aware that their eyesight is far superior to his own.
To proceed with this narrative, I may say that four
or five forts were built on the edge of the river
opposite the enemy's town, and distant not above
fifty or sixty yards. Here our guns were removed, and
a fresh battery formed ready for a bombardment, and
fire-balls essayed to ignite the houses.

'At this time Sherif Jaffer, from Linga, arrived with
about seventy men, Malays and Dyaks of Balow.
The river Linga, being situated close to Seribas, and
incessant hostilities being waged between the two
places, he and his followers were both more active
and warlike than the Borneans; but their warfare
consists of closing hand to hand with spear and
sword. They scarcely understood the proper use
of firearms, and were of little use in attacking
stockades. As a negotiator, however, the Sherif bore
a distinguished part; and on his arrival a parley
ensued, much against Makota's will, and some
meetings took place between Jaffer and a brother

Sherif at Siniawan, named Moksain.   After ten days'
delay nothing came of it, though the enemy betrayed
great desire to yield.   This negotiation being at an
end, we had a day's bombardment, and a fresh treaty
brought about thus : Makota being absent in Sarawak,
I received a message from Sherif Jaffer and Pangeran
Subtu to say that they wished to meet me ; and on
my consenting they stated that Sherif Jaffer felt
confident the war might be brought to an end,
though alone he dared not treat with the rebels ; but,
in case I felt inclined to join him, we could bring it
to a favourable conclusion.   I replied that our habits
of treating were very unlike their own, as we allowed
no delays to interpose ; but that I would unite with
him for one interview, and if that interview was
favourable we might meet the chiefs at once and
settle it, or put an end to all further treating.
Pangeran Subtu was delighted with the proposition,
urged its great advantages, and the meeting, by my
desire, was fixed for that very night, the place
Pangeran Illudin's fort at Sekundis.   The evening
arrived, and at dark we were at the appointed place
and a message was despatched for Sherif Moksain.
In the meantime, however, came a man from Pangeran Subtu to beg us to hold no intercourse ; that the
rebels were false, meant to deceive us, and if they
did come we had better make them prisoners.   Sherif
Jaffer, after arguing the point some time, rose to
depart, remarking that with such proceedings he

would not consent to treat. I urged him to stay, but finding him bent on going I ordered my gig (which had some time before been brought overland) to be put into the water—my intention being to proceed to the enemy's kampong and hear what they had to say. I added that it was folly to leave undone what we had agreed to do in the morning because Pangeran Subtu changed his mind ; that I had come to treat, and treat I would. I would not go away now without giving the enemy a fair hearing. For the good of all parties I would do it—and if the Sherif liked to join me, as we proposed before, and wait for Sherif Moksain, good ; if not, I would go in the boat to the kampong. My Europeans, on being ordered, jumped up, ran out and brought the boat to the water's edge and in a few minutes oars, rudder and rowlocks were in her. My companions, seeing this, came to terms, and we waited for Sherif Moksain, during which, however, I overheard a whispering conversation from Subtu's messenger, proposing to seize him, and my temper was ruffled to such a degree, that I drew out a pistol, and told him I would shoot him dead if he dared to seize, or talk of seizing, any man who trusted himself from the enemy to meet me. The scoundrel slunk off, and we were no more troubled with him. This past, Sherif Moksain arrived, and was introduced into our fortress alone—alone and unarmed in an enemy's stockade, manned with two hundred men. His bearing was firm ; he ad-

vanced with ease and took his seat, and during the
interview the only sign of uneasiness was the quick
glance of his eye from side to side. The object he
aimed at was to gain my guarantee that the lives of
all the rebels should be spared, but this I had not in
my power to grant. He returned to his kampong,
and came again towards morning, when it was agreed
that Sherif Jaffer and myself should meet the Patingis
and the Tumangong, and arrange terms with them.
By the time our conference was over the day broke,
and we descended to our boats to have a little rest.

'On the 20th December we met the chiefs on the
river, and they expressed themselves ready to yield,
without conditions, to the rajah, if I would promise
that they should not be put to death. My reply
was that I could give no such promise ; but if they
surrendered, it must be for life or death, according to
the rajah's pleasure, and all I could do was to use
my influence to save their lives. To this they
assented after a while ; but then there arose the more
difficult question, how they were to be protected
until the rajah's orders arrived. They dreaded both
Chinese and Malays, especially the former, who had
just cause for angry feelings, and who, it was feared,
would make an attack on them directly their sur-
render had taken from them their means of defence.
The Malays would not assail them in a body, but
would individually plunder them, and give occasion
for disputes and bloodshed. Their apprehensions were

almost sufficient to break off the hitherto favourable
negotiations, had I not proposed to them myself to
undertake their defence, and to become responsible
for their safety until the orders of their sovereign
arrived. On my pledging myself to this they yielded
up their strong fort of Balidah, the key of their
position. I immediately made it known to our own
party that no boats were to ascend or descend the
river, and that any person attacking or pillaging the
rebels were my enemies, and that I should fire upon
them without hesitation.

'Both Chinese and Malays agreed to the propriety of
the measure, and gave me the strongest assurances of
restraining their respective followers ; the former with
good faith, the latter with the intention of involving
matters, if possible, to the destruction of the rebels.
By the evening we were in possession of Balidah, and
certainly found it a formidable fortress, situated on a
steep mound, with dense defences of wood, triple deep,
and surrounded by two enclosures, thickly studded on
the outside with *ranjaus*. The effect of our fire had
shaken it completely, now much to our discomfort,
for the walls were tottering and the roof as leaky as a
sieve. On the 20th December, then, the war closed.
The very next day, contrary to stipulation, the Malay
pangerans tried to ascend the river, and when stopped
began to expostulate. After preventing many, the
attempt was made by Subtu and Pangeran Hassim
in three large boats, boldly pulling towards us.

Three hails did not check them, and they came on, in spite of a blank cartridge and a wide ball to turn them back. But I was resolved, and when a dozen musket balls whistled over and fell close around them, they took to an ignominious flight. I subsequently upbraided them for this breach of promise, and Makota loudly declared they had been greatly to blame, but I discovered that he himself had set them on.

'I may now briefly conclude these details. I ordered the rebels to burn all their stockades, which they did at once, and deliver up the greater part of their arms, and I proceeded to the rajah to request from him their lives. Those who know the Malay character will appreciate the difficulty of the attempt to stand between the monarch and his victims. I only succeeded when, at the end of a long debate—I soliciting, he denying—I rose to bid him farewell, as it was my intention to sail directly, since, after all my exertions in his cause he would not grant me the lives of the people, I could only consider that his friendship for me was at an end. On this he yielded. I must own that during the discussion he had much the best of it ; for he urged that they had forfeited their lives by the law, as a necessary sacrifice to the future peace of the country ; and argued that in a similar case in my own native land no leniency would be shown. On the contrary, my reasoning, though personal, was, on the whole, the best for the rajah and the people. I explained my extreme reluctance to have the blood

of conquered foes shed ; the shame I should experience
in being a party, however involuntarily, to their exe-
cution, and the general advantage of a merciful line of
policy. At the same time I told him that their lives
were forfeited, their crimes had been of a heinous
and unpardonable nature, and that it was only from so
humane a man as himself, one with so kind a heart,
that I could ask for their pardon ; but, I added, he
well knew that it was only my previous knowledge of
his benevolent disposition, and the great friendship I
felt for him, which had induced me to take any part
in the struggle. Other stronger reasons might have
been brought forward, which I forbore to employ,
as being repugnant to his princely pride, viz., that
severity in this case would arm many against him,
raise powerful enemies in Borneo proper, as well as
here, and greatly impede the future right government
of the country. However, having gained my point, I
was satisfied.

‘ Having fulfilled this engagement, and being, moreover, with many of my Europeans, attacked with ague,
I left the scene with all the dignity of complete success. Subsequently the rebels were ordered to deliver
up all their arms, ammunition and property ; and last,
the wives and children of the principal people were
demanded as hostages and obtained. The women and
children were treated with kindness and preserved
from injury or wrong. Siniawan thus dwindled
away. The poorer men stole off in canoes, and were

scattered about, most of them coming to Kuching. The better class pulled down the houses, abandoned the town and lived in boats for a month when, alarmed by the delay in settling terms and impelled by hunger, they also fled—Patingi Gapoor, it was said, to Sambas, and Patingi Ali and the Tumangong amongst the Dyaks. After a time it was supposed they would return and receive their wives and children. The army gradually dispersed to seek food, and the Chinese were left in possession of the once renowned Siniawan, the ruin of which they completed by burning all that remained and erecting a village for themselves in the immediate neighbourhood. Sherif Jaffer and many others departed to their respective homes, and the pinching of famine succeeded to the horrors of war. Fruit, being in season, helped to support the wretched people, and the near approach of the rice harvest kept up their spirits.'

Thus ended the great civil war, which is so renowned in local history. The three chiefs mentioned —Patingi Gapoor, Patingi Ali and the Tumangong— with their sons and relatives, will appear again as some of the principal actors in the history of Sarawak. All except Patingi Gapoor remained faithful to the end, or are still among the main supports of the present Government. I knew them all, with the exception of Patingi Ali, who was killed whilst gallantly heading an attack on the Sakarang pirates during Captain Keppel's expedition in 1844.

CHAPTER III

PEACE being again restored to the country, Brooke was enabled to study the position. Muda Hassim occasionally mentioned his intention of rewarding his English ally for his great services by giving him the government of Sarawak ; but nothing came of it, as when the document for submission to the Sultan was duly prepared it proved to be nothing but 'permission to trade.' However unsatisfactory this might be,

Brooke accepted it for the moment, and it was agreed that he should proceed to Singapore, load a schooner with merchandise, and return to open up the resources of the place. In the meantime the rajah was to build a house for his friend, and prepare a shipload of antimony ore as a return cargo for the schooner.

While in Singapore Brooke wrote to his mother concerning his plans, and he now added, 'I really have excellent hopes that this effort of mine will succeed; and while it ameliorates the condition of the unhappy natives, and tends to the promotion of the highest philanthropy, it will secure to me some better means of carrying through these grand objects. I call them grand objects, for they are so, when we reflect that civilisation, commerce and religion may through them be spread over so vast an island as Borneo. They are so grand, that self is quite lost when I consider them; and even the failure would be so much better than the non-attempt, that I could willingly sacrifice myself as nearly as the barest prudence will permit.'

Many, perhaps, could write such words, but Brooke really felt them, and fully intended to carry out his views, whatever obstacles might stand in his way; and they were many, for on his return to Sarawak in the *Royalist*, with the schooner *Swift* laden with goods for the market, he found no house built and no cargo of antimony ready. A house in Sarawak could be built in ten days or a fortnight, as the materials are all found in the jungle and the natives are expert at the work.

The antimony was procurable, but, as Brooke afterwards found, it was the product of forced labour, almost always unpaid. One cannot but smile at Brooke's first attempt at trade. Without sending up to see whether the antimony was ready, he accepted Muda Hassim's word, and then handed over to him the whole of the cargo of the *Swift*. What might have been expected followed. No sooner had the Malay rajah secured the goods than the most profound apathy was shown as to the return cargo. The same system was followed with regard to the government of the country; every attempt to discuss it was evaded, and I believe that Makota did his best to persuade Muda Hassim that the Englishman was but a bird of passage, who would soon get tired of waiting, and would sail away without the return cargo, and drop all thoughts of governing the country.

Pangeran Makota, who had been Brooke's enemy throughout all these proceedings, was now ready to act. He knew that the Land Dyaks in the interior, as well as the Malays of Siniawan whom the Englishman had aided to subdue, now looked to him as their protector; he therefore determined to destroy his prestige. He invited the Seribas Sea Dyaks and Malays to come to Sarawak ; they came in a hundred bangkongs, or long war boats, with at least three thousand men, with the ostensible object of attacking a tribe living near

the Sambas frontier, who had not been submissive
enough to Bornean exactions; but every violent act
they committed would have been overlooked if they
only gave a sufficient percentage of their captives to
the nobles. Already these wild devils had received
the rajah's permission to proceed up the river; the
Land Dyaks, the Malays, the Chinese were full of fear,
as all are treated as enemies by the Scribas when out
on the warpath. As soon as Brooke received notice
of what Muda Hassim, instigated by Makota, had
done, he retired to the *Royalist* and prepared both his
vessels for action. The Malay rulers, hearing how
angry he was, and uncertain what steps he might
take, recalled the expedition, which returned, furious
at being baulked of their prey, and would have liked
to have tried conclusions with the English ships, but
found them too well on their guard.

This very act which Makota expected would lower
the Englishman's prestige, naturally greatly enhanced
it, as it was soon known, even into the far interior, that
the white stranger had but to say the word and this
fearful scourge had been stayed.

Another event soon followed which greatly raised
Brooke's influence among the natives. He received
notice that an English vessel had been wrecked on
the north coast of Borneo, and that the crew were
detained as hostages by the Sultan of Borneo for the
payment of a ransom. He now sent the *Royalist* to
try and release them, whilst he despatched the *Swift*

to Singapore for provisions, and remained with three companions in his new house in Sarawak. Could anything better prove his cool courage? The *Royalist* failed in its mission, but almost immediately after its return, an East India Company's steamer came up the river to inquire as to its success, and finding the captive crew still at Brunei, proceeded there and quickly effected their release. The appearance of the *Diana* twice in the river had its effect on the population, as it was probably the first steamer they had ever seen.

Makota had been greatly disappointed that his intrigues had failed to force the white strangers to quit the country, but his fertile invention now thought of more sure and criminal means. 'Why not poison them?' He tried, but failed; his confederates confessed, and then Brooke resolved to act. Either Makota or himself must fall. By a judicious display of force, quite justified under the circumstances, he freed the rajah from the baneful influence of Makota, who from that time forward ceased to act as chief adviser, and regained his former ascendency. Muda Hassim immediately carried out his original promise, and in a formal document handed over the government of the district of Sarawak to Brooke. The news was received with rejoicing by the Land Dyaks, the Sarawak Malays and the Chinese, but with some misgivings by the rascally followers of the Bornean rajahs. This event took place in September 1841.

Brooke's first act was to request Muda Hassim to
return to their families the women and children who
had been given as hostages after the close of the
civil war.   He succeeded in most cases, but as the
younger brothers of Muda Hassim had honoured with
their notice some of the unmarried girls, he was
forced to leave ten of them in the harems of the
rajahs.

Being now Governor of Sarawak, he determined to
effect some reforms.   One of the greatest difficulties
he encountered was the introduction of impartial
justice ; to teach the various classes that all were
equal before the law.   He opened a court, at which
he himself provided, aided moreover, by some of the
rajah's brothers and the chiefs of the Siniawan
Malays, and dispensed justice according to the native
laws, which in most cases are milder than those
of European countries.   When absent himself his
chief officer acted for him.   As long as these laws
were only applied to Dyaks, Chinese or inferior
Malays, there was no resistance, but when the
privileged class and their unscrupulous followers were
touched, there arose some murmurings.

Brooke saw at once that to ensure stability to his
rule he must govern the people through, and with the
aid of, the chiefs to whom they were accustomed.
He therefore proposed to Muda Hassim to restore to
their former positions the men who had been at the
head of the late rebellion, and who certainly had been

www.ingramcontent.com/pod-product-compliance
Lightning Source LLC
Chambersburg PA
CBHW020731100426
42735CB00038B/1875